HAWKS

Tim Harris

Grolier
an imprint of

www.scholastic.com/librarypublishing

Published 2008 by Grolier
An imprint of Scholastic Library Publishing
Old Sherman Turnpike, Danbury,
Connecticut 06816

© 2008 Grolier

For The Brown Reference Group plc
Project Editor: Jolyon Goddard
Copy-editors: Lesley Ellis, Lisa Hughes,
    Wendy Horobin
Picture Researcher: Clare Newman
Designers: Jeni Child, Lynne Ross,
    Sarah Williams
Managing Editor: Bridget Giles

Volume ISBN-13: 978-0-7172-6237-3
Volume ISBN-10: 0-7172-6237-5

**Library of Congress
Cataloging-in-Publication Data**

Nature's children. Set 1.
    p. cm.
  Includes index.
  ISBN-13: 978-0-7172-8080-3
  ISBN-10: 0-7172-8080-2
  1. Animals--Encyclopedias, Juvenile.
  QL49.N38 2007
  590--dc22

                    2007018358

Printed and bound in China

PICTURE CREDITS

Front Cover: NHPA: Tom Kitchin
& Vicki Hurst.

Back Cover: Nature PL: Dietmar Nill,
Artur Tabor; Shutterstock: Ronnieoward.

Ardea: Duncan Usher 2–3, 33; **FLPA**:
Ron Austing 10, Franz Kovacs/Foto Natura
5, Chris Schenk/Foto Natura 17, Roger
Wilmshurst 38; **Nature PL**: Dietman Nill
18, Tom Vezo 46; **NHPA**: Brian Hawkes 42,
Mike Lane 4, 13, 37; **Photolibrary.com**:
Lynn D. Odell 30, Charles Palek 41;
Shutterstock: Caleb Foster 9, Patrick
Hermans 22, Jeffrey M. Horler 6, Ronnie
Howard 1, 29, 34, Willie Linn 14, 26–27,
Martin Nemec 21; **Still Pictures**: Charles
O. Slavens 45.

Contents

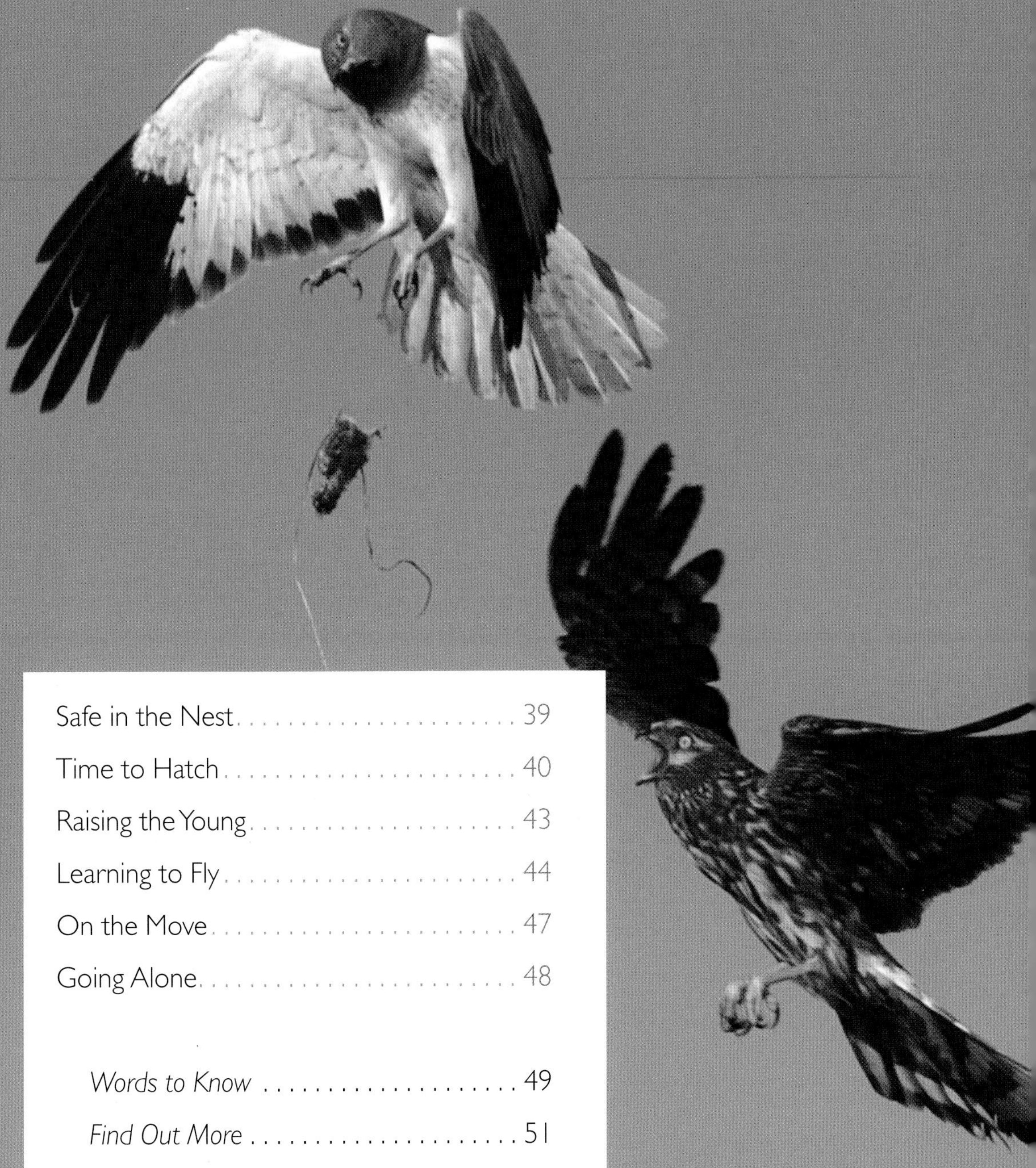

FACT FILE: Hawks

Class	Birds (Aves)
Order	Birds of prey (Falconiformes)
Families	Hawks (Accipitridae) and falcons (Falconidae)
Genera	Many worldwide; nine in North America (accipiters, buteos, falcons, harriers, and osprey)
Species	Many worldwide; 24 North American species
World distribution	Every continent apart from Antarctica
Habitat	Most types, from desert to rain forest, and from prairie to city
Distinctive physical characteristics	Darker back and lighter underside; hooked beak; strong talons; usually dull feathers and yellow legs
Habits	Active during the day; eat prey whole
Diet	Small mammals, snakes, frogs, birds, and large invertebrates

Introduction

Do you know which bird is the fastest in the world? It's a hawk called a peregrine falcon. All hawks are powerful, fast flyers. Some hawks can spend hours gliding in the sky hardly flapping their wings. And still others can hover, as if held up by an invisible string.

Hawks form a large group of birds of **prey**. Birds of prey hunt and eat other birds, mammals, fish, and large bugs.

A male sparrowhawk surveys his surroundings from a perch.

A red-tailed hawk lands on a tree's top branches. This hawk nests in woods near open country.

Hawk Highlights

Hawks are famous for their eyesight, which is eight to ten times more powerful than a human's. It's so good that from high in the air, a hawk can see the movements of tiny animals in the grass hundreds of feet below.

Hawks breed every year. They make good parents. Hawks build a nest in a tree, on the ground, or on a cliff. A female hawk usually lays between three and five eggs. The eggs **hatch** after about a month. Newly hatched hawks cannot walk or fly. They are covered in **down** and their eyes are open. The parents spend many weeks feeding and caring for their chicks. The chicks can fly after 30 to 50 days.

All Over the World

Hawks live in any place they can find food. Some prefer to hunt over grasslands, others prefer forests, and still others live in cities. Hawks live in every **habitat** in North America, from coastal marshlands to the highest peaks of the Rocky Mountains. Some hawks live in the far north of Alaska, and there are others on the Gulf Coast of Texas. Hawks live on every continent apart from Antarctica. But they do not live over the world's oceans.

Some hawks have more than one home. They mate, build a nest, and raise their young in one place. In winter they travel to a warmer place where there is more food.

You can find hawks
in towns and cities.
This one lives in
Pittsburgh.

After spotting prey, this young red-tailed hawk goes in for the kill.

A Family of Hawks

The family tree of the North American hawks has several different branches. The main branches are the accipiters (AK-SI-PA-TERS), falcons, and buteos. Accipiters are sometimes called bird-hawks because they hunt other birds. Their short, blunt-end wings help them twist and turn around trees as they chase birds through dense forest.

Falcons also chase other birds but have a very different shape. They have narrow, pointed wings and a long, thin tail. Falcons can fly very quickly, and they usually hunt over open areas.

The buteos have broad wings. They often fan out their tail feathers as they **soar** high in the air, looking for small mammals rummaging around on the ground below. Buteos eat fewer birds than either accipiters or falcons.

Feather Colors

Most hawks are not colorful birds. In fact, the brightest parts of most hawks are their yellow legs. Hawks also have a patch of yellow skin called a **cere** (SIR) at the base of the beak. The cere is difficult to see unless the bird is very close. Some falcons have a dark mark under each eye. Together these marks look like a drooping mustache.

Hawks' feathers are mostly shades of bluish gray or brown. The upperparts of a hawk are usually darker than the underside. The underside often has a pattern of bars, speckles, or streaks. Some hawks have patches of brighter feathers. For example, the red-tailed hawk has an orange-red tail. The American kestrel has a bright reddish brown back. And the Aplomado falcon has a red patch on its belly.

The Aplomado falcon lives in Central and South America. It has brighter feathers than most other hawks.

13

Also called the fish
hawk, the osprey is the
largest hawk and has an
impressive wingspan.

Small and Large

The osprey is the largest of the North American hawks. Its body is 23 inches (59 cm) long. Its wingspan stretches more than 5 feet (1.5 m) from tip to tip. That's long! An adult osprey weighs 3.5 pounds (1.6 kg).

At the other end of the scale, an American kestrel has a body just 9 inches (22 cm) long. But its wingspan is more than twice that length at 22 inches (55 cm). This fast-flying bird weighs just 4.1 ounces (117 g). That's the same weight as a small orange. Female hawks are generally a little bit larger than the males.

Mastery of the Air

Each kind of hawk has its own special flying skills. Some can glide and soar for long periods over great distances with only occasional wing beats. Other hawks must flap fast to fly but are skilled at twisting and turning quickly.

When the Sun heats up the air near the ground, the warmed air rises like an invisible balloon. As it gets higher, this warm, rising air becomes a doughnut-shaped column of air called a **thermal**. When a hawk flies into a thermal, the bird can soar and climb higher in the sky without even flapping its wings.

Rough-legged hawks and American kestrels can hover over the ground a bit like miniature helicopters. This skill lets them find prey—such as mice—before they dive down and pounce. When a merlin (a type of falcon) chases a small bird across an open prairie, the merlin follows every little movement of its intended dinner.

A rough-legged
hawk hovers
on a thermal.

A peregrine falcon
flies in search
of prey—usually
another bird such
as a songbird,
duck, or dove.

The Fastest Hawk

The peregrine falcon is the fastest bird in the world. Peregrines hunt fast-flying pigeons. Instead of chasing the pigeons in level flight, peregrines fly very high, then dive down on their prey. The peregrines dive—or **stoop**—very fast. Their stoop has been measured at up to 200 miles per hour (320 km/h). That's faster than most sports cars can speed!

To reach this speed, the peregrine dives almost vertically downward with its wings folded close to its body. A stooping peregrine looks more like a missile than a bird. Peregrines have a system of plugs that close off their **nostrils** as they stoop. These plugs control the amount of air that is taken into the lungs. Once the attack is made the peregrines grab the prey with their sharp **talons**.

Super Sight

Have you heard the expression that someone has "eyes like a hawk"? That's because hawks do have fantastic eyesight. A soaring hawk can see the movement of a mouse or frog on the ground hundreds of feet below. A peregrine falcon can see a flying pigeon from more than 1 mile (1.6 km) away.

A hawk's eyes are on the front of its head, like those of many other animal hunters. That lets the bird judge distances with pinpoint accuracy. Of course, without its amazing eyes, a hawk would struggle to catch its dinner. With such good eyesight, hawks have little need for a keen sense of smell. Hawks do have good hearing, though.

A falcon's sharp
eyesight is vital
for hunting prey.

The dull brown feathers of a hawk match the bark of trees.

Hide and Seek

Hawks work very hard at catching their prey. But their prey also work very hard at not getting caught. If prey animals see a hawk coming, they hide as quickly as they can. So the hawk must sneak up on its prey very fast, without alarming it.

The hawk's coloring is useful in keeping it hidden. Hawks spend much of their time perched in trees, waiting for the right moment to take off and attack a bird or mammal. The barred and speckled feathers of a hawk's underside and the unpatterned feathers of its back blend in very well with the bark of trees. If the hawk remains still, it becomes almost invisible until it's time to strike. And when a hawk flies overhead, its light underside almost matches the color of the sky—so animals on the ground do not easily see the hawk.

On the Menu

People have favorite foods, and so do hawks. Every type of hawk has a meal that it likes best. But if the hawk can't find its favorite food, it hunts for something else to eat.

Accipiters and falcons feast mostly on small birds they catch while flying. The northern goshawk sometimes chases, catches, kills, and eats much larger prey, such as a hare or even an owl. And gyrfalcons often kill ducks and even geese. Smaller hawks pounce down to grab large beetles, grasshoppers, and small lizards on the ground. Other hawks—especially the buteos—dine on small mammals, such as rodents and hares, again by pouncing on them from the air.

Hawks do not always get the meal they choose. One peregrine was watched by a scientist for a whole summer in the United States. It caught nine out of ten birds that it went after. But another peregrine observed in Australia was successful only three times out of ten.

Hunting Tricks

Whatever their choice of food, all hawks have one thing in common: they all hunt during daytime. But hawks catch their prey in many different ways. Sharp-shinned hawks and northern goshawks chase birds through the forest, twisting and turning to avoid trees. Two merlins sometimes hunt as a pair. They fly very close to the ground until they scare another bird into the air. Then one of the merlins follows every move of its prey until it catches up and kills it. Both merlins get to eat their victim.

Peregrines fly very high in the air until they see a meal. Then they stoop down and catch it. Most buteos soar, with wings outstretched, high over the ground until they see food they can swoop down on. Ospreys fly high over a lake, looking for a fish in the water below. When an osprey sees the shape of a trout or perch, the bird plunges into the water and pulls the fish out with its strong talons.

An osprey soars
away, holding
a freshly caught
fish in its talons.

Talons and Toes

On each foot a hawk has four strong toes with sharp claws, called talons. Three toes point forward, and the fourth points back. The fourth toe helps the hawk grip tight when it is perched on a branch.

The talons of a hawk are the weapons it uses for grabbing hold of its prey. People once thought that hawks clenched their toes like a fist to hit their prey. It is now known that all four extended talons strike the victim. The hawk stretches out its long legs and drives its supersharp talons into the unlucky mammal or bird. If that doesn't kill its prey, the hawk uses its other weapon—its sharp beak—to bite into its victim's neck.

A hawk's sharp claws—or talons—can tear through the skin of prey and hold it in a tight grip.

The sharp edge of a hawk's beak can chop up prey into small pieces.

Sharp Beak

If a hawk catches a small lizard, it can probably swallow it whole. However, bigger prey has to be broken up before it can be swallowed. We chew our food before we swallow, but birds do not have teeth. They use their sharp-edged, curved beak to tear the meat into pieces small enough to eat.

Of course, hawks do not have knives and forks to separate the meat from the bone. The hawk plucks the feathers from a bird meal, but everything else is swallowed. There are some bits of the animal that the hawk cannot digest, such as fur and bones. Those are sorted from the edible parts of the prey in the hawk's stomach. The fur and bones are later coughed up as **pellets**.

Courtship Displays

Male and female hawks pair up and mate each year in the early spring. Many pairs perform courtship displays to seal their partnership. Some act out spectacular flying displays.

Northern harriers have some of the most exciting displays. They fly around in circles, swoop down steeply, and then fly up equally steeply before diving down again. Male harriers show off by catching a small mammal or bird, then feeding it to their partner—in the air! The male flies over the female with the food in his talons, and the female flies up toward her partner. Then the male drops the food from his talons and the female catches it in hers.

Other hawk pairs swoop toward each other in midair. They clasp each other's talons for a few seconds, tumbling down toward the ground before releasing each other.

A male harrier
woos his mate
by dropping her
some prey.

Ospreys raise their chicks in huge nests built of sticks.

Stacks of Sticks

Female hawks must have a nest in which they can lay their eggs. The nest must be in a safe place and close to a supply of food. Most hawks build an isolated nest high up in a tree. But there are as many kinds of nests as there are hawks.

Ospreys' nests are the biggest hawk nests. They are huge piles of sticks that the birds collect and stack one on top of another. An osprey nest may be 10 feet (3 m) across and 10 feet deep. In some places people have encouraged these birds to nest by placing a cartwheel on top of a pole. The ospreys use the cartwheel as a platform on which to stack the sticks.

Some hawks cannot be bothered to build their own nest. They simply take over the nest of another large bird, such as a crow. Or they may steal the twigs and branches from another bird's nest to make their own.

Unusual Nests

Gyrfalcons and peregrines build their nests very high up on cliff ledges. Because there is no chance of **predators** getting to these places, the hawks may not bother with a nest at all. The female simply lays her eggs on the ledge.

In recent years, peregrines have started to nest on city "cliffs," that is, ledges on the sides of tall buildings. These ledges are just right for the peregrines because large numbers of pigeons live in cities, and peregrines—and their chicks—just love pigeons for their dinner!

Not all nests are built high up: harriers and merlins build their nests on the ground. And not all nests are on their own. Lesser kestrels, which live in Europe, are colonial nesters: several pairs build their nests close together, forming a colony. These birds often build their nests, which they return to year after year, on the towers of churches or on other tall buildings where they cannot be disturbed.

Peregrines nest on cliff ledges, where the eggs and chicks are safe from predators.

A pair of
sparrowhawks
builds a nest
in the branches
of a conifer tree.

38

Safe in the Nest

Hawks mate very early in spring, just before food becomes more plentiful after the harsh days of winter. After a female hawk lays her eggs in the nest, the lifestyle of both parents changes greatly.

The eggs must be kept warm, or the growing chicks within them will die. The only way to keep the eggs warm is for the mother or father—or both—to sit on them. Female hawks lose some of the feathers on their breast when they lay their eggs. They place their bald patch on the eggs, so more of their body heat passes to the growing offspring.

If prey is abundant, a female rough-legged hawk may lay up to seven eggs. If food is hard to find, however, she might lay only two eggs. The female alone incubates the eggs. Goshawk mothers lay two or three eggs, but both parents take turns keeping the eggs warm. How does the sitting bird eat while it is warming its eggs? Its partner brings food back to the nest for it.

Time to Hatch

About 30 or 35 days after the eggs are laid, the young birds are strong enough to hatch. Usually, an egg is laid every other day, so the chicks don't all hatch at the same time. The gap between the hatching of each egg helps the parents because, just like a human baby, newly hatched hawks need food from the moment they are born.

Baby hawks are called chicks. They are quite helpless when they first emerge into the world. Barely able to lift their own head, they are covered in soft, weak feathers called down. Unlike some birds, however, hawk chicks can open their eyes.

Sometimes, only the mother finds food to feed to her chicks, but usually both parents join in. They rip meat into tiny pieces to feed to the **nestlings**. If the weather is cold or if it starts to rain, the parents crouch over the chicks to keep them warm and dry.

These red-tailed hawk chicks need food—and lots of it—as soon as they hatch.

A sparrowhawk
mother warms
and protects
her chicks.

42

Raising the Young

When it is about a week old, a hawk chick is strong enough to hold up its head and shout for food. It squeals loudly to make sure its parents know that it is hungry. This is a tough time for the parents. Their chicks have to eat their own body weight in food every day. The adults have to hunt all day to find enough food for their chicks' breakfast, lunch, and dinner. The parents still have to tear the meat, but now the young hawks can swallow larger pieces than in their first week out of the egg.

When dinner is easy to find, all this hard work pays off and the chicks quickly grow strong. But that is not always the case. The parents do their best, but if food is hard to find, the last-hatched babies might starve to death.

If an animal comes close to the nest, the parents screech to scare it away. If the intruder continues to approach, the adults attack with their sharp talons and beak.

Learning to Fly

As we have seen, adult hawks and falcons are complete masters of the skies. But you would not believe that if you ever saw a young hawk learning to get airborne. By the age of about 30 days, the young hawks have grown strong wing feathers, but the birds don't really know how to use their wings. At first, they flap their wings without leaving the nest. Then they glide to the branch of a nearby tree. Finally, the **fledglings** make their first proper flight—but they still don't look very confident. Sometimes they crash-land on the ground!

A rough-legged hawk can usually fly about 40 days after emerging from its egg. This time is called the **fledging period**. For Cooper's hawks the fledging period is about 30 days, and for ospreys it is about 50 days. Luckily, the parents keep a watchful eye on their progress. The young birds cannot be left alone until they are comfortable in the air and can catch their own food.

A red-shouldered hawk fledgling tries out its new wings.

The Cooper's hawk migrates as far south as Mexico when food becomes scarce during winter.

On the Move

Many hawks spend part of the year in one place and part somewhere else. Why is that? In some places in the far north there is plenty of prey to catch in summer, but conditions become very harsh during winter. Most of the hawks' food disappears in the fall. Many of the small birds that the hawks hunt fly south to warmer conditions, and many mammals **hibernate** for winter.

Rather than starve, thousands of hawks move south in September and October. They often travel together on a **migration** that lasts several weeks. The young birds migrate as well as the adults. Some fly from Canada to the United States. Others fly even farther, to Mexico, the Caribbean, or South America. The hawks make stops on the way, to feed and rest. But they don't stop for winter until they get to an area where there is plenty of food.

Going Alone

A young hawk's life becomes very tough once
it is left to look after itself. To start, it must
quickly become a skilled hunter. If it does
not eat a regular meal, it will starve to death.
Unlike many birds, which can simply peck at
seeds or leaves to get their dinner, a hawk's
food—another bird or a mammal—moves
and has to be chased.

A young hawk also has to learn how to spot
danger. Hawks do not have many enemies, but
larger hawks and owls sometimes kill smaller
hawks, so the young bird has to remain watchful.
This may be especially difficult if the bird is
tired and hungry after a long migration. But if
the young bird can make it through its first fall
and winter, it stands a good chance of living
until it is 10 years old or more. During those
years the hawk will be able to raise several
families of its own.

Words to Know

Cere	A patch of yellow skin at the base of a hawk's beak.
Down	Very soft, fine feathers.
Fledging period	The time it takes from hatching to learning to fly.
Fledglings	A young bird that has grown its first adult feathers.
Habitat	The area in which an animal or plant lives.
Hatch	To break out of an egg.
Hibernate	To spend winter in a deep sleeplike state.
Migration	A long journey from one place to another, generally to breed or find food.

Nestlings	Birds that have not yet left the nest.
Nostrils	Openings at the base of the beak that let in air.
Pellets	Parts of prey—such as fur and bones—that cannot be digested. Pellets are coughed up by birds of prey.
Predators	An animal that hunts other animals for food.
Prey	An animal that is hunted by another animal for food.
Soar	To rise high in the sky by using air currents and not wing beats.
Stoop	A fast dive by a bird of prey.
Talons	A bird of prey's sharp claws.
Thermal	A doughnut-shaped column of warm, rising air.

Find Out More

Books

Hickman, P. *Birds of Prey Rescue*. Richmond Hill,
Ontario, Canada: Firefly books, 2006.

Warhol, T. *Hawks. Animalways*. Tarrytown, New York:
Benchmark Books, 2005.

Web sites

Hawks Aloft, Inc.
www.hawksaloft.org/kids.html
Games, experiments, and interesting
facts about hawks.

The Peregrine Fund
www.peregrinefund.org
Lots of information about peregrine
falcons and other birds of prey.

Index